Julie R

PUBLISHED B

Copyright © 2017 A

Contents

Introduction

"Mmmmmm...Doughnuts" – Homer Simpson

Homer Simpson may not be the most smartest of characters, but when it comes to the topic of doughnuts, he can rightly be considered both an expert and a true connoisseur. I very much hope that by the end of this collection of the best 50 doughnut recipes, then you too will consider yourself the same.

The doughnut is a relatively easy creation to make, yet hard to rival in its comforting look, texture, warmth and taste. It is a food we see everywhere, a comforting treat that we enjoyed in our childhood and a dessert or snack that remains appealing and attractive no matter how old you are.

Despite often looking intricate and complex, doughnuts are not difficult to make yourself. You don't need any particular equipment. They use ingredients you probably have in your cupboard now. If you can follow a few instructions on a recipe and use a scale, then the job is almost done. Pleasingly, doughnuts also offer much scope for your imagination and creative powers to be put to good use to make a dish that is both wonderful to taste and beautiful to behold.

One of the oldest questions in the realm of doughnuts concerns its form. Do you opt for the yeast doughnuts which can be deep-fried or cake doughnuts which are baked? The history of both are rich, however I have always preferred to create doughnuts which are baked for two reasons. Most importantly, to me they taste better and secondly, they are much easier and quicker to make.

For those two reasons, the vast majority of the recipes in this book are for baked doughnuts. There are a couple of doughnuts I have included that should be fried, such as the hard to resist drop doughnuts, but most of the recipes in this book are baked. Much of this is personal choice of course and there is no definitive right or wrong answer. However, if you've always tried fried doughnuts, I urge you to give the baked ones a good try as I am sure you would love them as well!

Just before you start baking your doughnuts, do read my top 8 doughnut baking tips to avoid some of the mistakes I have made myself. I hope they save you time and will allow you to get the best possible results as quickly as you can.

Enjoy reading this collection of doughnut recipes – by the end of this book, you will be an expert in the wonderful and warming delicacy of the baked doughnut.

Happy baking!

Julie

Top 8 Doughnut Making Tips

1.) The instructions for these recipes call for the ingredients to be mixed, however take care not to overmix them. Once they are just about combined, then leave the dough as it is.

2.) When adding the glaze, ensure that the doughnut has cooled completely. If you are applying a thicker glaze, the doughnut will need to be room temperature. You could also consider making double or treble the amount of glaze required. It will be fine in the refrigerator for months and can easily be used for the next batch.

3.) If you are adding sugar or cinnamon sugar to the cooked doughnuts, then do it when the doughnuts are still warm. The heat will make the sugar stick all over the doughnut. I often like to roll my doughnuts in melted, warm butter before applying the sugar coating.

4.) Grease and flour your doughnut pan. I mention this in the recipes, but it bears repeating as it's important. Ensure you have a good quality doughnut pan and grease it before you add the dough. This is a good first step to take before making the doughnuts so it's ready to go as soon as you need it. Greasing and flouring the pan will avoid leaving part of the doughnut inside the pan and ensure waste and mess are minimized.

5.) Be generous with your portion of dough. I tend to fill the cavity of the doughnut pan to the top or perhaps four fifths full to give the doughnut a proper size and feel. Your oven may vary a little so experiment yourself of course, but it's normally far better to have more mixture for a doughnut than less.

6.) Watch your baking times. You want to avoid overbaking doughnuts as they can go dry. You will get to know the right times very quickly, but you can always test them by inserting a toothpick into the middle of the doughnut. If it comes out with just a couple of crumbs on and slightly moist, that's ideal. The doughnut will continue to cook for a while even when removed from the heat.

7.) When adding your topping or glaze there are a couple of ways of doing it. I tend just to turn the doughnut upside down and dip it right into the glaze before returning to a wire rack. However, if you would like a slightly more precise way of doing it, then add the glaze to a piping bag or just a small bag with the corner cut off. You can use the same technique to add the mixture into the doughnut pan as well.

8.) Be patient and enjoy the process! There will probably be a few errors along the way and not every baked doughnut is going to end in total triumph. They won't take long to perfect, but experimenting for yourself along the way with different flavors, ingredients and ideas is a great way to becoming the perfect creator of doughnuts. Keep trying and innovating along the way!

Equipment

One of the joys of making baked doughnuts is the lack of specialist equipment that is required. Certain foods like the waffle will require a waffle iron to be used, however there is no such need for a beautiful batch of doughnuts.

You will need a good quality doughnut pan (or two), a couple of mixing bowls, a good-sized wire ack for cooling purposes, perhaps a piping bag or two for the mixture and the glaze and an oven of course, but that is all that is needed. The chances are, you may already have all the above in your kitchen already.

Do ensure when purchasing a doughnut pan that it is of a good quality, coated and non-stick. They will enable you to get your cooked doughnuts out more easily as well as making the washing-up a far more pleasant experience. You can experiment with the size and number of cavities in each. You can also buy mini-doughnut pans which can be a lot of fun to use, especially for children's parties where a larger doughnut might prove too much and go to waste. All the recipes here can be adapted into mini-doughnuts with the right pan. I normally stick to metal doughnut pans, but I know people who have had lots of success with silicone based doughnut pans as well.

Weights and names

I've used cups as my measurement of choice as that's what I was brought up with and am used to, but if you prefer ounces or grams, then 1 cup of all-purpose flour or confectioners' sugar (used for the glaze) is about 4 ¼ ounces or 125 grams.

1 cup of white sugar is about 200 grams. If you prefer to use brown sugar, that is a little more with 1 cup being 220 grams. I tend to measure butter (unsalted) in tablespoons. 8 tablespoons are half a cup which weighs about 112 grams.

The names for virtually all the ingredients in this book are the same throughout the world, perhaps with a few exceptions. All-purpose flour is also known as plain flour. Confectioners' sugar or powdered sugar is icing sugar. Baking soda is the same as bicarbonate of soda. Graham Crackers are digestive biscuits. Half and half cream is the same as single cream.

Free Gift

I would love to send you an entirely free gift – my Top 100 Cupcake Recipes. This is a whole book dedicated to the wonderful world of cupcakes and contains 100 fantastic, easy to make recipes. If you would like to get a free copy, then just follow the link below and I'll get it out to you straightaway!

Just visit here - http://eepurl.com/bWd-XL - for a free copy of the Top 100 Cupcake Recipes!

Cupcake Cookbook

TOP 100 CUPCAKE RECIPES

Julie Brooke

Almond Doughnuts

Ingredients

2 cups all-purpose flour

½ cup sugar

1 teaspoon almond extract

1 ½ teaspoons baking powder

½ teaspoon baking soda

1 cup milk

2 eggs

½ teaspoon salt

½ teaspoon vanilla

4 tablespoons butter, melted

Topping

1 ½ cups confectioners' sugar

½ cup cocoa powder

4 tablespoons water

Coconut flakes

Instructions

Preheat oven to 350F. Add the flour, sugar, baking powder, baking soda and salt into a bowl and set aside. In a separate bowl, add the milk, almond extract, vanilla, eggs and butter and whisk. Add the contents of this bowl to the dry ingredients. Stir until combined.

Add the dough to the pre-greased doughnut pan and bake for about 12 minutes. Remove from the oven and let the doughnuts cool for 5 minutes in the pan. Then add them to a wire rack to cool completely.

While cooling, make the glaze by adding the sugar, cocoa powder and water to a bowl and mixing well. You can add a little more water if too thick or a little more sugar if too thin. Place the top of each doughnut into the glaze and return to wire rack. Sprinkle the coconut flakes or a favorite topping of your own, add to a plate and serve.

Apple Doughnuts

Ingredients

2 cups all-purpose flour

1 teaspoon baking powder

½ teaspoon baking soda

½ teaspoon nutmeg

1 teaspoon salt

1 cup sugar

1 teaspoon cinnamon

2 eggs

1 cup vegetable oil

1 cup apple, peeled and grated

Topping

1 cup sugar

1 teaspoon cinnamon

¼ cup melted butter

Instructions

Preheat oven to 350F. Add the flour, baking powder, baking soda, sugar, nutmeg, cinnamon and salt into a bowl mix. In a different bowl, add the eggs and oil and whisk. Add the wet ingredients to the dry and mix until just combined. Fold in the apply gently. Add the mixture to your pre-greased doughnut pan and bake for 12-14 minutes. Remove from the oven and allow to cool for two minutes before removing to a wire rack.

For the important topping, you can either use shop-bought cinnamon sugar or make your own easily by combining the sugar and cinnamon. Dip the doughnuts into the melted butter and cover in sugar to serve warm. Delicious with a hot drink, these will disappear fast!

Banana Doughnuts

Ingredients

2 cups flour

1 teaspoon baking powder

½ teaspoon baking soda

½ teaspoon nutmeg

½ teaspoon cinnamon

1 cup mashed bananas

2 eggs

½ cup sugar

½ cup vegetable oil

2 tablespoons milk

½ teaspoon vanilla

Cinnamon sugar

Instructions

Preheat oven to 350F. Add the baking powder, baking soda, nutmeg, cinnamon, sugar and flour into a bowl and mix together. In a separate bowl, add the bananas, eggs, vegetable oil, milk and vanilla and mix together. Add the wet ingredients into the bowl with the dry ingredients and mix until just combined.

Spray the doughnut pans and spoon in the mixture. Bake for around 12 minutes or until golden brown. Remove to cool for five minutes on a wire rack and cover in cinnamon sugar to serve.

Blueberry Doughnuts

Ingredients

2 1/2 cups all-purpose flour

1 cup sugar

1 teaspoon vanilla

½ teaspoon baking soda

½ teaspoon baking powder

½ teaspoon salt

2 eggs

½ cup butter

1 cup blueberries (thawed from frozen or fresh)

Cinnamon sugar

¼ cup melted butter

Instructions

Preheat oven to 350F. Add the flour, sugar, baking powder, baking soda and salt to a bowl. In a separate bowl, add the eggs, melted butter, vanilla and whisk together. Add the wet ingredients to the dry and mix until just combined. Fold in the blueberries.

Add the dough to the greased doughnut pan and bake for about 10 minutes. Remove from the oven and let them sit in the doughnut pan for two minutes before removing to a wire rack to cool. Dip them in melted butter and roll around in cinnamon sugar before serving.

Buttermilk Doughnuts

Ingredients

1 cup buttermilk

½ cup sugar

1 egg

3 cups all-purpose flour

1 teaspoon baking soda

1 teaspoon baking powder

½ teaspoon salt

½ teaspoon nutmeg

½ teaspoon cinnamon

¼ cup butter, melted

Oil for frying

Glaze

1 cup confectioners' sugar

½ teaspoon vanilla

3 tablespoons milk

Instructions

Add the buttermilk, sugar and egg into a bowl and whisk. In a separate bowl, add the flour, salt, nutmeg, cinnamon, baking powder and baking soda and mix. Add the wet ingredients to the dry and mix together. Knead the mixture to create a soft dough consistency.

Flour the surface and spread out the dough to about ¼ inch thick. Cut the doughnuts out with a 3-inch cutter. Heat the oil in a skillet, add the doughnuts and cook until golden brown. Remove to drain.

To make the glaze, add the sugar, vanilla and milk into a bowl and mix. You can add more milk or sugar to get the right consistency. Once the doughnuts have drained and cooled, add the glaze and serve.

Butterscotch and Chocolate Doughnuts

Ingredients

1 ½ cups all-purpose flour

½ cup sugar

2 egg

1 teaspoon vanilla

1 ½ teaspoon baking powder

½ teaspoon baking soda

½ teaspoon salt

½ cup milk

1 cup butterscotch chips

½ cup chocolate chips

Glaze

1 ½ cups confectioners' sugar

½ teaspoon vanilla

3 tablespoons milk

¼ cup butterscotch chips

Instructions

Preheat oven to 350F. Add the flour, sugar, baking powder, baking soda and salt to a bowl and set aside. In a separate bowl, add the sugar, milk, vanilla and eggs and whisk. Add the wet ingredients to the dry and mix until just combined. Fold in the butterscotch chips and the chocolate chips together. Add the dough to a pre-greased doughnut pan and bake for 12-14 minutes. Remove from the oven and let the doughnuts sit in the pan for a couple of minutes before removing to a wire rack.

While the doughnuts are cooling, make the glaze. Add the sugar, vanilla and milk to a bowl and mix well. Take each cooled doughnut and dip the top into the glaze. Return to a plate and then scatter further butterscotch chips on the glaze as it sets before serving.

Cake Doughnuts

Ingredients

½ cup sugar

4 cups flour

1 tablespoon baking powder

1 teaspoon salt

1/2 teaspoon nutmeg

½ teaspoon cinnamon

2 eggs

1 cup milk

¼ cup butter, melted

1 teaspoon vanilla

Oil for frying

Cinnamon sugar

Instructions

Add the sugar, baking powder, salt, cinnamon, nutmeg and flour into a bowl and mix together. In a separate bowl, add the milk, butter, eggs and vanilla and whisk together. Add the wet ingredients to the dry and mix. Once you have covered the bowl, place in the fridge for at least 2 hours.

Remove the dough from the fridge and roll out so it's about half an inch think. Cut out a circle with a cutter of about 3 inches. Use a much smaller one or a bottle cap to cut the inner circle.

Heat the oil in a heavy skillet. Drop the doughnuts into the heated oil, keep turning them over until golden brown. Remove from heat to drain. Coat them in cinnamon sugar and serve.

Caramel Doughnuts

Ingredients

1 ½ cups all-purpose flour

½ cup sugar

1 teaspoon baking powder

½ teaspoon salt

1 egg

1 teaspoon vanilla

¾ cup milk

½ cup melted butter

Glaze

1 cup brown sugar

½ cup heavy cream

1 teaspoon kosher salt

1 teaspoon vanilla

2 tablespoons butter

Instructions

Preheat oven to 350F. Add the flour, baking powder, sugar and salt into a bowl, mix and set aside. In a separate bowl, add the egg, milk, vanilla and butter and whisk. Add the wet ingredients to the dry and mix until just combined. Add the dough to the pre-greased doughnut pan and cook for about 10 minutes. Let them cool in the pan and then remove to a wire rack.

To make the glaze, add the sugar and a little water into a saucepan over medium heat. The sugar will begin to boil. Don't stir. Once it goes a caramel color, remove from the heat and slowly add the cream, vanilla and butter. Add the saucepan back to the heat, stir in the salt and remove from the heat to cool. Add the top of the doughnuts to the warm caramel and add a little salt to the top to serve.

Carrot Cake Doughnuts

Ingredients

1 ½ cups all-purpose flour

½ cup sugar

1 teaspoon cinnamon

¾ teaspoon baking powder

½ teaspoon salt

2 eggs

1/3 cup vegetable oil

½ cup grated carrot

½ cup milk

1 teaspoon vanilla

Frosting

1 packet cream cheeses (3 oz.)

2 tablespoons milk

½ cup powdered sugar

Instructions

Preheat oven to 350F. Add the flour, sugar, salt, cinnamon and baking powder into a bowl and whisk together. In a separate bowl, add the eggs, oil, milk, carrot and vanilla and whisk. Add the dry ingredients to the wet and mix. Spoon in the mixture into the doughnut pan, cook for 10 minutes and remove to cool.

While the doughnuts are cooling, make the frosting. Beat the cream cheese, milk and powdered sugar together until smooth. An electric mixer is easiest. I prefer just a little powdered sugar, but if not sweet enough, add another ½ cup. Once the doughnuts have cooled off, then spread a liberal serving of the frosting over the top and serve.

Chai Doughnuts

These are lovely and spicy. You can try all sorts of different spices and varying amounts, but this is my favorite combination.

Ingredients

2 cups all-purpose flour

½ cup sugar

2 eggs

1 teaspoon cinnamon, ground

1 teaspoon cardamom, ground

1 teaspoon ginger, ground

½ teaspoon nutmeg

½ teaspoon salt

1 teaspoon baking powder

½ teaspoon baking soda

1 teaspoon vanilla

4 tablespoons butter, melted

½ cup milk

½ cup plain yogurt

Topping

1 cup sugar

1 teaspoon cinnamon

1 teaspoon cardamom

½ teaspoon ginger

½ cup butter, melted

Instructions

Preheat oven to 350F. Add the flour, baking powder, baking soda cinnamon, cardamom, ginger, nutmeg and salt to a bowl and mix together. In another bowl, add the butter, milk, sugar, vanilla, yogurt and eggs and whisk together. Add the wet ingredients to the dry and mix until just combined.

Add the dough to the pre-greased doughnut pan and bake for about 10 minutes. Remove from the oven, let them cool for a couple of minutes and then remove to a wire rack to cool further.

Make the glaze by adding the sugar, cinnamon, cardamom and ginger to a bowl and mixing well. Take each doughnut and dip it wholly into the melted butter before rolling it in the topping mix. Add to a plate and serve.

Cherry Doughnuts

Ingredients

2 cups all-purpose flour

1 cup sugar

1 teaspoon baking powder

1 teaspoon baking soda

½ teaspoon salt

2 eggs

1 teaspoon vanilla

1 cup buttermilk

½ cup melted butter

20 maraschino cherries, chopped

Juice from the chopped cherries

Glaze

2 cups confectioners' sugar

1 teaspoon cherry extract

½ cup half and half cream

Instructions

Preheat oven to 350F. Add the flour, baking powder, baking soda, salt and sugar to a bowl and mix. In a separate bowl, add the eggs, vanilla, buttermilk, any juice from the chopped cherries and butter and whisk. Add the wet ingredients to the dry and mix until just combined. Fold in the chopped cherries. Bake for about 10 minutes. Remove and let them cool in the pan for a couple of minutes, before removing to a wire rack.

Add the sugar, cherry extract and glaze to a bowl and mix. When you are happy with the consistency, dip in the doughnuts and apply your favorite topping to serve.

Chocolate and Avocado Doughnuts

Avocadoes seem to have made their way into every recipe these days which is great for me as I love them. Fortunately, they go very well in doughnuts as well as this recipe shows.

Ingredients

1 ½ cups all-purpose flour

1 cup sugar

2 eggs

1 teaspoon vanilla

1 medium-sized avocado, well mashed

2 teaspoons baking powder

½ teaspoon baking soda

½ cup cocoa powder

½ teaspoon salt

1 cup milk

Topping

½ ripe avocado, mashed

1 cup confectioners' sugar

½ teaspoon vanilla

3 tablespoons milk

Instructions

Preheat oven to 350F. Add the flour, baking powder, baking soda, cocoa and salt into a bowl and set aside. In a different bowl, mash the avocado, add the sugar and mix. Add in the eggs, milk and vanilla and mix again. Add the dry ingredients to the wet and mix until just combined. Add the dough to the doughnut pan and cook for 12 minutes. Let them cool for a while once removed and then add to a wire rack.

To make the topping, add all the ingredients together and mix well. You can add a little more water or milk if you prefer if too thick or more sugar if too runny. Dip the cooled doughnuts in and serve.

Cinnamon Doughnuts

Ingredients

2 cups all-purpose flour

1 cup sugar

1 teaspoon baking powder

½ teaspoon salt

1 egg

1 teaspoon vanilla

1 teaspoon cinnamon

¼ cup melted butter

1 cup whole milk

Cinnamon sugar

Instructions

Preheat oven to 350F. Add the flour, sugar, cinnamon and baking powder to a bowl and mix. In a separate bowl, add the egg, butter, milk and vanilla. Add the wet ingredients to the dry and stir until just combined.

Add the dough to the pre-greased doughnut pan and bake for 15 minutes. Let them cool in the pan for a couple of minutes and then remove to a wire rack. Melt a little more butter and dip the doughnuts in fully so they are entirely coated. Roll the warm doughnuts in the butter and then into the cinnamon sugar. Add to a platter and serve warm. These are wonderful with a lovely cup of coffee or tea. They also go very well with children's parties, though I tend to make mini version as the larger ones are just a bit too big.

Coconut Doughnuts

Ingredients

2 cups all-purpose flour

½ cup sugar

1 ½ teaspoons baking powder

½ teaspoon baking soda

½ teaspoon salt

1 cup coconut milk

2 eggs

1 cup shredded coconut

½ cup vegetable oil

1 teaspoon vanilla

Glaze

1 cup confectioners' sugar

2 tablespoons coconut milk

½ teaspoon vanilla

Instructions

Preheat oven to 350F. Add the flour, sugar, baking powder, baking soda and salt to a bowl and set aside. In a new bowl, add the eggs, coconut milk, vegetable oil and vanilla and whisk together. Add the wet ingredients to the dry and mix in. Fold in the cup of shredded coconut.

Add to the pre-greased doughnut pan and cook for 10-12 minutes. Remove and allow to cool in the pan for two minutes before removing to a wire rack. Make the glaze in the meanwhile by mixing the sugar, coconut milk and vanilla. Add a little water if too thick or more sugar if too thin. Dip the cooled doughnuts into the glaze and add a little more shredded coconut to the top or sprinkles or your own favorite topping to serve.

Coffee Doughnuts

Ingredients

1 cup all-purpose flour

½ cup coffee, room temperature

½ teaspoon instant coffee

1 teaspoon baking powder

½ teaspoon baking soda

¼ teaspoon salt

1 teaspoon vanilla

1 egg

¼ cup vegetable oil

½ cup sugar

Glaze

2 cups confectioners' sugar

1 teaspoon vanilla

3 teaspoons instant coffee

Boiling water

Instructions

Preheat oven to 350F. Add the flour, baking powder, baking soda, instant coffee, salt and sugar into a bowl. In a separate bowl, add the egg, vegetable oil, vanilla and coffee and whisk together. Add the wet ingredients to the dry and mix until just combined.

Add the mixture to a greased doughnut pan and bake for about 12 minutes. Remove to cool on a wire rack for a couple of minutes. Make the glaze by pouring a little boiling water over the instant coffee until it dissolves. Add the sugar and vanilla and stir until dissolved. Add more water or sugar depending on the desired consistency. Dip the doughnuts into the glaze and return to the rack to set and serve.

Confetti Doughnuts

These look adorable and are wonderful for parties for children (or adults as well!). Don't hold back on the decoration of these – less is definitely not more for once.

Ingredients

2 cups all-purpose flour

½ teaspoon salt

1 cup sugar

2 teaspoons baking powder

½ teaspoon baking soda

1 cup milk

3 tablespoons butter

2 eggs

1 teaspoon vanilla

½ cup sprinkles

Glaze

2 cups confectioners' sugar

1 teaspoon vanilla

3 tablespoons milk

More sprinkles (or topping of your choice)

2 drops food coloring (pink is traditional choice for these doughnuts).

Instructions

Preheat oven to 350F. Add the flour, salt, baking powder and baking soda into a bowl and set aside. Add the eggs, milk, butter, sugar and vanilla into a bowl and whisk well. Add the wet ingredients to the dry and mix until just combined. Add the sprinkles and fold in to the mixture.

Add the dough to the pre-greased doughnut pans and cook for about 10 minutes. Remove and let the doughnuts cool in the pan for a couple of minutes before removing to a wire rack. Let them cool further while you make the glaze. Add the sugar, food coloring and vanilla together and gradually add in the milk while continuing to mix until a good consistency is reached. Dip the cooled doughnuts into the pink glaze, return to the plate and then add a generous handful of sprinkles over the glaze while still setting to serve.

Dark chocolate Doughnuts

Wonderfully indulgent, these chocolate doughnuts make a rich treat.

Ingredients

1 ¾ cups all-purpose flour

½ cup sugar

½ cup cocoa powder, unsweetened

½ teaspoon espresso powder

1 teaspoon vanilla

1 egg

1 cup vegetable oil

½ teaspoon salt

1 teaspoon baking soda

Glaze

2 cups confectioners' sugar

4 tablespoons cocoa

1 teaspoon vanilla

2 tablespoons milk

Instructions

Preheat oven to 350F. Add the flour, cocoa powder, baking soda, espresso powder and salt to a bowl and set aside. In a separate bowl, add the vanilla, egg and oil and whisk together. Add the wet ingredients to the dry and mix until just combined. Add the dough to the doughnut pan and bake for about 12 minutes. Remove from the oven, allow to cool for a couple of minutes and then remove to a wire rack.

While cooling, make the glaze by adding all the ingredients into a bowl and mixing well. Add in more milk if a little thick and whisk. Dip each doughnut into the glaze and add your favorite topping or serve as they are.

Drop Doughnuts

I'm generally more of a fan of baked doughnuts than fried just for ease of making and taste, but these drop doughnuts are special. So easy to make, they taste delicious and wonderful served warm and covered in cinnamon.

Ingredients

1 ½ cups all-purpose flour

½ cup sugar

2 eggs

1 teaspoon vanilla

2 teaspoons baking powder

½ teaspoon salt

½ cup milk

4 tablespoons vegetable oil

Additional oil for cooking

Cinnamon sugar

Instructions

Add the flour, sugar, baking powder and salt to a bowl and set aside. In a separate bowl, add the vanilla, eggs, oil and milk together and whisk. Add the wet ingredients to the dry and mix until just combined. Heat the oil up to 350F.

Now drop a teaspoon of mixture into the heated oil. Keep turning and when golden brown on all sides, remove to place on wire rack to drain. When they have cooled slightly, roll them in the cinnamon sugar and serve warm.

Eggnog Doughnuts

I've tried many things for the perfect Christmas breakfast and these would feature every time. But don't just keep them for the one day – they're great for parties in the festive season. Get Christmas started early with these amazing eggnog doughnuts.

Ingredients

2 cups all-purpose flour

½ cup sugar

1 ½ teaspoons baking powder

½ teaspoon baking soda

½ teaspoon cinnamon

½ teaspoon salt

¼ teaspoon nutmeg

1 cup eggnog

1 teaspoon vanilla

2 eggs

4 tablespoons butter, melted

Glaze

2 cups confectioners' sugar

1 teaspoon vanilla

3 tablespoons milk

Instructions

Preheat oven to 350F. Add the flour, baking powder, baking soda, cinnamon, salt and nutmeg to a bowl and set aside. Add the sugar, eggs, vanilla, butter and eggnog to a separate bowl and whisk together. Add the dough to the pre-greased doughnut pan and bake for about 8 minutes. Remove the doughnuts, allow them to cool in the pan and then place on a wire rack.

Add the sugar and vanilla to a bowl and add milk. Mix until the right consistency is reached adding more milk to make the glaze thinner if needed. Dip the cooled doughnuts into the glaze and place on a platter to serve.

Ginger Doughnuts

Ginger is often associated with Christmas and is an evocative smell, but these really should be eaten all year around!

Ingredients

2 cups all-purpose flour

2 teaspoons baking powder

½ teaspoon baking soda

1 teaspoon cinnamon

2 teaspoons ground ginger

½ teaspoon salt

½ cup brown sugar

1 teaspoon vanilla

2 eggs

½ cup milk

3 tablespoons butter, melted

Glaze

1 cup confectioners' sugar

1 tablespoon butter

2 tablespoons milk

2 teaspoons ground ginger

Instructions

Preheat oven to 350F. Add the flour, baking powder, baking soda, cinnamon, salt and ginger to a bowl and set aside. In another bowl, add the vanilla, eggs, milk, sugar and butter and whisk together. Add the wet ingredients to the dry and mix until just combined.

Add the dough to the pre-greased doughnut pan and bake for about 10 minutes. Remove from the oven and after cooling in the pan for a couple of minutes, remove to a wire rack. Make the glaze by adding the ingredients into a bowl and mixing well. Drizzle over the cooled doughnuts, add a topping of your choice and serve.

Honey Doughnuts

Simple and light, these are ideal for breakfast. They're not overpowering and will keep you going for a busy morning.

Ingredients

2 cups all-purpose flour

2 teaspoons baking powder

½ teaspoon baking soda

½ teaspoon cinnamon

½ teaspoons salt

½ cup sugar

2 eggs

4 tablespoons butter, melted

1 cup buttermilk

5 tablespoons honey

1 teaspoon vanilla

Glaze

2 cups confectioners' sugar

3 tablespoons honey

2 tablespoons milk

Instructions

Preheat oven to 350F. Add the flour, baking powder, salt, baking soda and cinnamon to a bowl and set aside. In a different bowl, add the sugar, eggs, buttermilk, butter, vanilla and honey and whisk together. Add the wet ingredients to the dry and mix until just combined. Add the dough to a doughnut pan and bake for about 10 minutes. Let them cool for two minutes in the pan, before removing to a wire rack.

While they are cooling, make the glaze. Add the ingredients to a bowl and whisk together. Add a liberal helping of the glaze to the top of the doughnuts and serve.

Ice Cream Doughnuts

These make a great summer treat. Use whatever flavour of ice-cream you like of course. I normally go for plain vanilla, with a chocolate topping on top

Ingredients

2 cups all-purpose flour

1 cup sugar

1 teaspoon baking powder

½ teaspoon salt

1 egg

1 teaspoon vanilla

¼ cup melted butter

1 cup whole milk

Ice cream flavor of your choice

Topping

1 cup mini chocolate chips

2 tablespoons butter

½ teaspoon vanilla

Sprinkles or topping of your choice

Instructions

Preheat oven to 350F. Add the flour, sugar and baking powder to a bowl and mix. In a separate bowl, add the egg, butter, milk and vanilla. Add the wet ingredients to the dry and stir until just combined.

Add the dough to the pre-greased doughnut pan and bake for 15 minutes. Let them cool in the pan for a couple of minutes and then remove to a wire rack. Once the doughnuts have cooled completely, cut each in half.

Take a scoop of ice-cream and add it the bottom half. Try to aim for a flatter layer rather than a proper "scoop" so you can make a sandwich with the top layer. You may find it easier to use a smaller spoon to take several scoops rather than one large one. Add the top layer, press down gently and return to the freezer while you make the chocolate topping.

Heat the chocolate chips up either in a microwave or in a glass bowl above boiling water. Take out the doughnuts and add as much chocolate topping as you would like. Sprinkle your favorite topping on generously and serve for a cool and refreshing treat.

Jelly-filled Doughnuts

Ingredients

2 teaspoon dry yeast (1 packet)

2/3 cup warm water

1 ¾ cups all-purpose flour

½ cup sugar

½ teaspoon salt

3 tablespoons butter, melted

2 egg yolks

1 cup jam, raspberry or your own choice

Topping

2 tablespoons butter, melted

½ cup confectioners' sugar

Instructions

Preheat oven to 350F. Add the flour, sugar, salt and yeast into a bowl, followed by the warm water, egg yolks, butter and vanilla. Beat the mixture for a couple of minutes or until it is all combined. You can do this by hand, but an electric mixer would be far easier. Add it to a floured surface and knead it for 30 turns. Add it back to the bowl and cover it. Leave for at least 10 minutes or until the dough has risen.

Add a good amount of flour to a surface as the dough is quite sticky and roll out to about ½ inch thick. Using a 2 ½ inch cutter, add the circles to a baking sheet covered in parchment paper. Place a towel over the baking sheet and leave somewhere warm for an hour.

Place in the oven and cook for about 15 minutes. Remove them from the oven, cover in the melted butter and roll in the sugar before placing on a wire rack to cool. Fill a pastry bag with the jam of your choice and feed in a generous amount to each doughnut before serving.

Key Lime Doughnuts

These have a lovely, tangy lime flavour to them that will brighten up any day!

Ingredients

2 cups all-purpose flour

1 ½ teaspoons baking powder

½ teaspoon baking soda

½ teaspoon salt

1 egg

½ cup buttermilk

½ cup vegetable oil

1 teaspoon vanilla

1 tablespoon key lime juice

2 teaspoons key lime zest

Glaze

1 ½ cups confectioners' sugar

½ teaspoon vanilla

3 tablespoons key lime juice

Crushed grahams crackers

(Warm water if required)

Instructions

Preheat oven to 350F. Add the flour, baking powder, salt and baking soda to a bowl and set aside. In another bowl, add the sugar, key lime juice and zest, buttermilk, vanilla, vegetable oil and egg and whisk together. Add the wet ingredients to the dry and mix until combined.

Add the dough to the greased doughnut pan and bake in the oven for 10 minutes. Remove to cool in the pan for a couple of minutes before placing on a wire rack to cool down completely. To make the glaze, add the ingredients to a bowl and mix until combined. You can use a little more juice or even just water to make the glaze thinner if needed. Dip the cooled doughnut in the glaze, sprinkle with the crushed crackers and return to a platter to set and then serve.

Lemon Doughnuts

Ingredients

2 cups all-purpose flour

2 teaspoons baking powder

½ teaspoon salt

2 eggs

½ cup sugar

1 teaspoon vanilla

½ cup butter

½ cup buttermilk

Zest of 3 lemons

Glaze

2 cups confectioners' sugar

Lemon juice (from the 3 lemons used for the zest)

Instructions

Preheat oven to 350F. Add the flour, baking powder, salt and sugar into a bowl. In a separate bowl, add the eggs, vanilla, butter, buttermilk and zest and mix together. Add the wet ingredients to the dry and mix until just combined. Add the dough to the pre-greased doughnut pan and bake for about 10 minutes. Let them cool in the pan for a couple of minutes and remove to a wire rack.

For the glaze, simply whisk the sugar and lemon juice and dip the doughnuts in to serve.

Mango Doughnuts

Ingredients

2 cups all-purpose flour

1 cup sugar

2 eggs

½ cup butter, melted

1 teaspoon cinnamon

1 teaspoon vanilla

½ teaspoon salt

2 teaspoons baking powder

½ cup vegetable oil

1 cup sugar

1 cup mango puree

Mango Puree

2 mangoes, chopped and diced finely

½ cup sugar

2 tablespoons water

Glaze

2 cups confectioners' sugar

½ cup mango puree

1 teaspoon vanilla

1 tablespoon hot water

Instructions

Preheat oven to 350F. Add the flour, cinnamon, baking powder and salt into a bowl and set aside. In another bowl, add the sugar, eggs, oil, butter and vanilla and whisk together. Add the wet ingredients to the dry and mix until just combined. You can use shop-bought mango puree, but it is easy enough to make your own. Add the mangoes, sugar and water to a blender and puree until a lovely smooth texture is reached. Fold in a cup of the puree to the mixture.

Add the dough to the doughnut pan and bake for about 15 minutes. Remove from the oven and leave the doughnuts to cool in the pan for 2 minutes. Remove to a wire rack to cool. Make the glaze by adding ½ cup of puree to the sugar and vanilla with a little water and mixing until the right consistency is achieved. Dip the top of the doughnut into the glaze and serve.

Maple Bacon Doughnuts

The classic fusion of sweet and salty is summed up in these treats below. These maple bacon doughnuts make the perfect breakfast and are lovely with a hot cup of coffee.

Ingredients

2 cups all-purpose flour

½ cup sugar

2 teaspoons baking powder

½ teaspoon cinnamon

1 teaspoon salt

½ cup milk

2 eggs

1 teaspoon vanilla

3 tablespoons butter

10-12 strips bacon, cooked and crumbled

Glaze

2 cups confectioners' sugar

½ teaspoon vanilla

1 cup maple syrup

2 tablespoons milk

Instructions

Preheat oven to 350F. Add together the flour, baking powder, cinnamon and salt to a bowl and mix. In a separate bowl, add the milk, eggs, sugar, vanilla and butter and whisk well. Add the wet ingredients to the dry and mix until just combined. Add to the pre-greased doughnut pan and bake for about 10 minutes. Remove and let them cool in the pan before removing them to a wire rack.

Make the glaze by adding all the glaze ingredients together and mixing well. Add a little more milk if too thick or more sugar if too thin. Dip the cooled doughnuts into the glaze and then add a liberal helping of the crushed bacon all over the glaze before it sets.

Matcha Doughnuts

If you've never tried matcha, then these doughnuts serve as a great introduction. And they look great too.

Ingredients

2 cups all-purpose flour

½ cup sugar

2 tablespoons matcha powder

2 teaspoons baking powder

½ teaspoon salt

1 teaspoon vanilla

1 cup milk

1 egg

2 tablespoons butter, melted

Glaze

1 ½ cups confectioners' sugar

½ teaspoon vanilla

2 teaspoons matcha powder

3 tablespoons of water

Instructions

Preheat oven to 350F. Add the flour, baking powder, sugar, salt and matcha powder to a bowl and set aside. Now add the vanilla, egg, milk and butter to another bowl and whisk together. Add the wet ingredients to the dry and mix until just combined. Add to the doughnut pan and bake for about 10 minutes. Remove from the oven, allow to cool for a couple of minutes and then transfer to a wire rack.

To make the glaze, mix all the ingredients together adding more sugar to make it thicker or more water to make it thinner. Dip the doughnuts into the glaze once they have cooled and add to a plate to be served.

Mint Choc Chip Doughnuts

Ingredients

2 cups all-purpose flour

½ cup cocoa powder

½ cup sugar

1 teaspoon baking powder

1 teaspoon baking soda

½ teaspoon salt

2 eggs

1 teaspoon vanilla

½ cup milk

1 cup mini chocolate chips

½ cup melted butter

Glaze

2 cups confectioners' sugar

1 teaspoon vanilla

3 tablespoons milk

½ teaspoon peppermint extract

Instructions

Preheat oven to 350F. Add the flour, cocoa powder, salt, baking powder and baking soda to a bowl and mix. In a separate bowl, add the sugar, milk, butter, eggs and vanilla and whisk. Add the wet ingredients to the dry and mix until just combined. Add in the chocolate chips and mix in.

Add the mixture to the pre-greased doughnut pans and cook for 10 minutes. Allow to cool for five minutes and remove to a wire rack to cool further.

To make the glaze, add all the ingredients to a bowl and mix, adding more sugar or milk to achieve the desired consistency. Dip the top of the doughnut in and add your favorite topping if required before serving.

Mocha Doughnuts

That combination of coffee and chocolate is hard to beat. Don't just drink a mocha though, make a doughnut out of it with the recipe below

Ingredients

2 cups all-purpose flour

2 cups sugar

½ teaspoon salt

2 teaspoons baking powder

½ teaspoon baking soda

1 teaspoon vanilla

3 eggs

1 cup milk

½ cup cocoa, unsweetened

½ cup coffee, brewed and cooled

1 cup chocolate chips

Glaze

2 cups confectioners' sugar

½ teaspoon vanilla

3 tablespoons coffee, brewed and cooled

Instructions

Preheat oven to 350F. Add the flour, baking powder, baking soda, salt and cocoa to a bowl, mix and set aside. In a separate bowl, add the vanilla, eggs, milk, sugar and coffee and whisk together. Add the wet ingredients to the dry and mix until just combined. Fold in the chocolate chips. Add the dough to the pre-greased doughnut pans and cook for about 12 minutes. Remove from the oven to cool in the pan for a couple of minutes, before placing on a wire rack to cool completely.

Make the glaze by adding the ingredients into bowl and mixing well. Add a little more water to the glaze if too thick. Dip the cooled doughnuts into the glaze and scatter a few mini chocolate chips over the top or leave as they are to serve.

Nutella Doughnuts

Ingredients

1 ½ cups all-purpose flour

½ cup sugar

1 teaspoon baking powder

½ teaspoon salt

1 egg

1 teaspoon vanilla

½ cup milk

½ cup Nutella

½ cup melted butter

Glaze

1 cups confectioners' sugar

2 tablespoons Nutella

1 tablespoon hot water

Your choice of topping

Instructions

Preheat oven to 350F. Add the flour, baking powder and salt together into a bowl. In a different bowl, add the sugar, Nutella, butter, egg and vanilla and whisk together. Add the wet ingredients to the dry and mix until just combined. Add the dough to a pre-greased doughnut pan. Bake for about 12 minutes, let them cool in the pan for a couple of minutes and finally place on a wire rack.

To make the glaze, add the ingredients to a bowl and mix together. Add more sugar or water to change to the desired consistency. Dip the doughnuts into the glaze and then top with sprinkles or hazelnuts or any topping of your choice.

Oatmeal Choc Top Doughnuts

Ingredients

2 cups oat flour

½ cup sugar

2 teaspoons baking powder

½ teaspoon baking soda

½ teaspoon salt

1 cup milk

1 teaspoon vanilla

2 eggs

4 tablespoons vegetable oil

Glaze

1 ½ cups confectioners' sugar

4 tablespoons cocoa powder

½ teaspoon vanilla

4 tablespoons water

Instructions

Preheat oven to 350F. You don't need to buy oat flour especially for this recipe. Just use a blender to grind oats at home. Add the oat flour, baking soda, baking powder and salt into a bowl and set aside. Now add the milk, vanilla, eggs, milk and sugar into a bowl and whisk. Add the wet ingredients to the dry and mix until combined.

Add the dough to your pre-greased doughnut pan and bake for about 10 minutes. Remove from the oven to sit for a couple of minutes before moving to a wire rack to cool. In the meanwhile, make the glaze. Add the glaze ingredients to a bowl and whisk together well. Add more sugar if too thin and more water (or milk if you prefer) if too thin. Pour over the cooled doughnuts, add a topping of your choice if you like and serve.

Orange Doughnuts

Ingredients

2 cups all-purpose flour

1 cup sugar

1 teaspoon baking powder

1 teaspoon baking soda

½ teaspoon salt

2 eggs

¼ cup butter

½ cup heavy cream

1 teaspoon vanilla

1/3 cup fresh orange juice

Zest of 2 oranges

Glaze

2 cups confectioners' sugar

1 teaspoon orange zest

1 tablespoon hot water

Instructions

Preheat oven to 350F. Add the flour, sugar, baking powder, baking soda and salt to a bowl and mix. In a different bowl, add the cream, butter, orange juice, eggs, vanilla and orange zest. Add the wet ingredients to the dry and mix until just combined.

Add the dough to the pre-greased doughnut pan and cook for about 10 minutes. Let them cool for a couple of minutes and then remove to rest on a wire rack. To make the glaze, whisk the sugar, orange zest and water together until the right consistency is reached. Dip the doughnuts into the glaze and serve.

Peanut Butter and Chocolate Doughnuts

Ingredients

1 cup all-purpose flour

½ cup sugar

1 egg

1 teaspoon vanilla

½ cup smooth peanut butter

1 teaspoon baking powder

¼ teaspoon baking soda

1/3 teaspoon salt

1/3 cup buttermilk

Glaze

½ cup semi-sweet chocolate chips

1 tablespoon unsalted butter

1 tablespoon milk

Instructions

Preheat oven to 350F. Add the peanut butter and sugar into a bowl and mix together. In a separate bowl, add the egg, vanilla and buttermilk and whisk together. Add to the peanut butter and sugar mixture. In another bowl, add the flour, baking powder, baking soda and salt and combine. Add the dry ingredients to the wet ingredients and mix until just combined.

Add the mixture to the pre-greased doughnut-pan. Bake for about 10 minutes, allow to cool a little and then place onto a wire rack. To make the glaze, add the chocolate chips, butter and milk into a bowl and microwave for 20 seconds. If not quite melted, continue to microwave 10 seconds at a time. Dip the doughnuts in to cover the top and then sprinkle on your favorite topping!

Pineapple Doughnuts

Ingredients

2 cups all-purpose flour

1 cup sugar

½ cup butter

1 egg

2 teaspoons baking powder

½ teaspoon salt

½ cup milk

¼ cup butter

½ teaspoon cinnamon

1 teaspoon vanilla

1 can (15 ounces) pineapple, sliced

Instructions

Preheat oven to 350F. Add the flour, ½ cup of sugar, baking powder, salt and cinnamon to a bowl and set aside. In a different bowl, add the butter, egg, milk and vanilla and whisk. Add the wet ingredients to the dry and mix until just combined.

Extract the pineapple slices and cut in half across the slice. Add the remaining sugar over the doughnut pan into each cavity. Add a slice of pineapple on the top of the sugar. Add the dough onto the pineapple and bake for about 10 minutes. Remove and let cool for a couple of minutes in the pan. Then remove the doughnuts from the pan and allow them to cool on a wire rack before serving warm.

Pistachio Doughnuts

Ingredients

2 cups all-purpose flour

2 teaspoons baking powder

½ teaspoon salt

1 cup sugar

1 cup pistachios, chopped

2 eggs

½ cup unsalted butter, melted

1 teaspoon vanilla

½ cup milk

Glaze

2 cups confectioners' sugar

½ teaspoon vanilla

2 tablespoons milk

Crushed pistachios

Instructions

Preheat oven to 350F. Using a food processor, grind the pistachios until they are very fine. Then add them to a bowl (hold back a teaspoon or two for the glaze) with the flour, baking powder and salt. In another bowl, add the butter, sugar, vanilla, milk and eggs and whisk together. Add the wet ingredients to the dry and mix until just combined. Add the dough to the doughnut pan and bake for 12-14 minutes. Leave them in the pan for a couple of minutes, before placing them on a wire rack.

Make the glaze by adding all the ingredients together and mixing in a bowl. Add more sugar or milk to make thicker or thinner for the right consistency. Dip the cooled doughnuts in the glaze and sprinkle a few crumbled pistachios on the top to serve.

Pumpkin Doughnuts

Ingredients

2 cups all-purpose flour

2 teaspoons baking powder

1 teaspoon salt

1 cup sugar

1 cup pumpkin puree

2 teaspoons pumpkin pie spice

3 eggs

1 teaspoon vanilla

½ cup unsalted butter, melted

1/3 cup vegetable oil

Topping

1 cup sugar

2 teaspoons ground cinnamon

1/3 cup unsalted butter melted

Instructions

Preheat oven to 350F. Add the flour, pumpkin pie spice, baking powder and salt into a bowl and mix together. In a separate bowl, add the puree, sugar, vegetable oil, butter eggs and vanilla and beat together. Add the dry ingredients into the wet ingredients bowl and beat again.

Add the mixture into your doughnut pan and cook for about 10 minutes. Remove when done and while cooling, prepare the topping. You can simply use cinnamon sugar if you prefer, but I like to combine the cinnamon and sugar, cover the doughnuts in melted butter and then dip them into the mixture. You can add a little more cinnamon or sugar to the mixture as well depending on preference.

Rainbow Doughnuts

These look, and taste, beautiful. Guaranteed to be a hit at any party, they are as much to make as they are to eat (well, almost anyway).

Ingredients

2 cups all-purpose flour

½ cup sugar

1 ½ teaspoons baking powder

½ teaspoon baking soda

1 teaspoon vanilla

2 eggs

½ teaspoon salt

4 tablespoons butter, melted

½ cup milk

Food coloring: yellow, green, blue, purple, orange and yellow

Glaze

2 cup confectioners' sugar

3 tablespoons milk

Sprinkles (lots!)

Instructions

Preheat oven to 350F. Add the flour, sugar, baking powder, baking soda and salt into a bowl and set aside. In a separate bowl, add the butter, milk, vanilla, eggs and whisk together. Add the wet ingredients to the dry and mix until just combined. Separate the mixture out to 6 smaller bowls and use the food coloring on each one.

Add the dough to the pre-greased doughnut pan with a portion from each bowl making a rainbow. Bake for about 10 minutes. Remove from the oven and let the doughnuts cool for 5 minutes in the pan. Then add them to a wire rack to cool completely.

While cooling, make the glaze by adding the sugar, vanilla and milk together. Use a little more milk if too thick or sugar if too thin. Take each doughnut and dip the top of it in the glaze. Put a liberal helping of sprinkles on and return to the plate to serve.

Raisin and Choc Chip Doughnuts

Ingredients

2 cups all-purpose flour

2 teaspoons baking powder

1 teaspoon baking soda

½ cup sugar

½ teaspoon salt

1 teaspoon vanilla

½ cup raisins

½ cup chocolate chips

1 cup milk

1 egg

4 tablespoons butter

Topping

2 cups confectioners' sugar

½ teaspoon vanilla

3 tablespoons milk

Additional chopped raisins or choc chips to taste

Instructions

Preheat oven to 350F. Add the flour, baking powder, baking soda and salt to a bowl and set aside. In a separate bowl, add the sugar, vanilla, milk, egg and butter into a bowl and whisk together. Add the wet ingredients to the dry and mix until just combined.

Add the dough to a pre-greased doughnut pan and cook for about 10 minutes. Remove from the oven, let the doughnuts cool in the pan for 2 minutes and then place on a wire rack to cool completely.

While they are cooling, make the glaze by adding the sugar, vanilla and milk to a bowl and mixing well. Take each cooled doughnut and dip the top into the glaze so it is fully covered. Return to a plate, cover in a further topping or chopped raisins or extra choc chips to taste and serve.

Raspberry and Lemon Doughnuts

Ingredients

2 cups all-purpose flour

2 teaspoons baking powder

½ teaspoon salt

3 tablespoons lemon juice

Zest of 1 lemon

1 tablespoon vegetable oil

1 egg

1 cup sugar

1 cup buttermilk

1 cup fresh raspberries

Glaze

2 cups confectioners' sugar

½ teaspoon vanilla

2 teaspoons lemon juice

1 tablespoon milk

Instructions

Preheat oven to 350F. Add the flour, baking powder and salt to a bowl and mix together. In a separate bowl, add the lemon juice, egg sugar, vegetable oil, lemon juice and buttermilk and lemon zest and whisk together. Add the wet ingredients to the dry and mix until just combined. Fold in the raspberries gently.

Add the batter to the doughnut pan and bake for 10 minutes. Remove to cool in the pan for a couple of minutes, before placing them on a wire rack. While they are cooling, make the glaze by add all the glaze ingredients to a bowl and mixing together. You can add more milk to dilute the glaze or more sugar to thicken it to reach the right consistency.

Dip the top of the doughnuts into the glaze and place on the wire rack to set and serve.

Red Velvet Doughnuts

Ingredients

1 ½ cups all-purpose flour

2 teaspoons cocoa powder

½ teaspoon baking soda

½ cup sugar

½ teaspoon salt

½ cup milk

1 teaspoon vanilla

2 eggs

½ teaspoon vinegar

½ cup vegetable oil

3 teaspoons red food coloring

Glaze

1 cups confectioners' sugar

1 teaspoon vanilla

1 tablespoon hot water

2 ounces' cream cheese

Instructions

Preheat oven to 350F. Add the flour, cocoa powder, baking soda, salt and sugar to a bowl and mix together. In a separate bowl, add the milk, eggs, oil, food coloring, vinegar and vanilla and whisk. Add the wet ingredients to the dry and mix until just combined.

Add the dough into the pre-greased doughnut pans. Cook for 10 minutes and then allow to cool in the pan for a couple of minutes. Remove to cool on a wire rack.

To make the glaze, add the sugar, vanilla cream cheese and water into a bowl and mix until combined. Spread the glaze evenly on the doughnuts and serve.

Rhubarb Doughnuts

I love the tartness of rhubarb combined in tandem with the sweetness of a doughnut rolled in cinnamon sugar. Rhubarb is a great ingredient, often overlooked, but try it with these doughnuts and you won't be disappointed.

Ingredients

2 cups all-purpose flour

1 ½ teaspoons baking powder

½ teaspoon baking soda

½ teaspoon salt

½ teaspoon cinnamon

1 teaspoon vanilla

2 eggs

½ cup vegetable oil

1 cup sugar

½ cup buttermilk

2 tablespoons butter

1 cup rhubarb, chopped and diced very finely

Topping

1 cup sugar

1 teaspoon cinnamon

¼ cup melted butter

Instructions

Preheat oven to 350F. Add the rhubarb and butter to a pan and cook over medium heat for 7-8 minutes or until the rhubarb is soft. Remove and allow to cool. Add the flour, baking powder, baking soda, cinnamon and salt to a bowl and set aside. In another bowl, add the sugar, eggs, vanilla, oil and buttermilk and whisk together. Add the wet ingredients to the dry and mix until just combined. Gently fold in the softened rhubarb.

Add the mixture to the doughnut pan and add to the oven for about 15 minutes. Remove and allow to cool a little, before removing to a wire rack. For the topping, add the cup of sugar and cinnamon together and mix. Dip the cooled doughnuts into the melted butter and then into the cinnamon sugar. Return to a platter to serve and be devoured!

S'Mores Doughnuts

Chocolate, roasted marshmallows followed with more chocolate and cracker crumbs. Yes, it's decadent but they're delicious and make a great treat for the kids (and you).

Ingredients

1 ½ cups all-purpose flour

1 cup sugar

½ cup cocoa powder, unsweetened

1 ½ teaspoons baking powder

½ teaspoon baking soda

½ teaspoon salt

½ cup milk

4 tablespoons butter. melted

½ cup plain yogurt

1 teaspoon vanilla

2 eggs

Filling / Glaze

1 cup crushed Graham crackers

1 cup mini marshmallows

1 cup chocolate chips

½ teaspoon vanilla

Instructions

Preheat oven to 350F. Add the flour, baking powder, baking soda, cocoa powder and salt into a bowl and mix together. In a separate bowl, add the eggs, vanilla, milk, yogurt, butter and sugar and whisk together. Add the wet ingredients to the dry and mix until just combined.

Add the mixture into the pre-greased doughnut pan and cook for about 10 minutes. Once removed from the oven, allow to cool in the pan for a couple of minutes before removing to a wire rack to cool completely. Cut each doughnut in half.

Gently melt the chocolate with the vanilla. Add the melted chocolate to the bottom half of the doughnut and then pack with marshmallows. Place the bottom half of the doughnut on a covered baking sheet and broil very briefly. When the marshmallows have started to melt, remove and add the top half of the doughnut. Cover the top with more melted chocolate and sprinkle the crushed Graham cracker crumbs all around. Add to a platter and serve.

Sour Cream Doughnuts

Ingredients

2 ½ cups all-purpose flour

1 teaspoon baking powder

1 teaspoon baking soda

1 teaspoon salt

½ teaspoon cinnamon

½ teaspoon nutmeg

½ cup sugar

½ cup butter, melted

2 eggs

1 teaspoon vanilla

½ cup sour cream

Oil for frying

Glaze

2 cups confectioners' sugar

1 teaspoon vanilla

3 tablespoons milk

Instructions

Add the flour, baking powder, baking soda, salt, cinnamon and nutmeg into a bowl and mix together. In a separate bowl, add the eggs, sugar, butter and vanilla and beat together. Gradually add the sour cream and beat again.

Add the wet ingredients to the dry and mix until combined. Cover the bowl and place in the fridge for two hours.

Heat the oil in a deep skillet. Dust a work surface and spread out the dough to around ½ an inch thick. Cut with a three-inch cutter and use a bottle top to cut out the inner circle. Add the doughnuts to the heated oil and cook until golden brown. Remove to drain and cool.

While the doughnuts are cooling, make the glaze. Add the confectioners' sugar, vanilla and milk together and mix until a suitable consistency is reached. Dip the doughnuts into the glaze and serve

Strawberry Doughnuts

Ingredients

2 cups all-purpose flour

1 cup sugar

1 teaspoon baking powder

1 teaspoon baking soda

½ teaspoon salt

2 eggs

1 teaspoon vanilla

1 cup buttermilk

½ cup melted butter

1 cup chopped strawberries

Glaze

2 cups confectioners' sugar

¼ cup chopped strawberries

1 tablespoon hot water

Instructions

Preheat oven to 350F. Add the flour, sugar, baking powder, baking soda and salt into a large bowl, mix and set aside. In another bowl, add the eggs, vanilla, buttermilk and butter and whisk. Add the wet ingredients to the dry and mix until just combined. Fold in the chopped strawberries. Bake for about 10 minutes. Remove and allow to cool in the pan for 2 minutes. Remove to a wire rack to cool.

To make the glaze, add the sugar, strawberries and water to a bowl. Mix until the right consistency is added. Add more sugar or water if you want to thicken or thin the glaze. Dip the top of the doughnuts in, return to the rack for 30 minutes and serve.

Sweet Potato Doughnuts

The title might sound surprising at first, but these are great. Give them a try for a pleasant surprise for yourself!

Ingredients

2 cups all-purpose flour

½ cup sugar

1 teaspoon cinnamon

2 teaspoons baking powder

½ teaspoon baking soda

1 teaspoon vanilla

½ teaspoon salt

2 eggs

1 cup milk

1 cup sweet potato – cooked and mashed

Sugar

Instructions

Preheat oven to 350F. Add the flour, sugar, baking powder, cinnamon, baking soda and salt into a large bowl and set aside. In a separate bowl, add the eggs, sweet potato, milk and vanilla and whisk well. Add the wet ingredients to the dry and mix until just combined.

Add to the doughnut pan and cook for about 10 minutes. Once you have removed them from the oven, let them sit in the pan for a couple of minutes and then transfer to a wire rack. Once they are cooler, dip and roll them in sugar to serve.

Vanilla Glazed Doughnuts

It's hard to beat the simplicity and beauty of vanilla in both doughnuts and ice cream in my opinion. These vanilla doughnuts are easy to create and will be gone just as quickly as the more exotic flavors as well!

Ingredients

2 cups all-purpose flour

2 teaspoons baking powder

½ teaspoon salt

4 tablespoons butter, melted

½ cup sugar

2 eggs

½ cup full fat milk

2 teaspoons vanilla

Glaze

1 cup confectioners' sugar

1 teaspoon vanilla

Pinch of salt

2 tablespoons milk

Instructions

Preheat oven to 350F. Add the flour, sugar, salt and baking powder to a bowl and set aside. Add the eggs, milk, vanilla and butter to another bowl and whisk together. Add the wet ingredients to the dry and mix until just combined. Add the dough to the pre-greased doughnut pan and place in the oven for about 10 minutes. Remove, allow to cool in the pan for a couple of minutes and then remove to a wire race.

While the doughnuts are cooling, make the glaze. Add all the ingredients for the glaze to a bowl and mix together. You can add more sugar to make it thicker or more milk (or water) to thin it out. Dip the cooled doughnuts into the glaze and then cover with your favorite topping or just leave as they are and serve once set.

Walnut and Banana Doughnuts

Ingredients

2 cups all-purpose flour

2 teaspoons baking powder

1 teaspoon baking soda

½ teaspoon salt

3 bananas, mashed

1 teaspoon vanilla

1 cup sugar

½ teaspoon cinnamon

1 egg

4 tablespoons butter, melted

1 cup walnuts, chopped

Topping

2 cups confectioners' sugar

½ teaspoon vanilla

3 tablespoons milk

¼ cup walnuts, chopped

Instructions

Preheat oven to 350F. Add in the flour, baking powder, baking soda, salt, cinnamon and sugar to a bowl and set aside. In another bowl, add the bananas, egg, vanilla and butter and mix together. Add the wet ingredients to the dry and mix again until everything is combined. Fold in the chopped cup of walnuts.

Add the dough to the pre-greased doughnut and bake for about 15 minutes. Remove the doughnuts and let them cool for 5 minutes, before transferring to a wire rack. To make the glaze, add the sugar, vanilla and milk into a bowl and stir well. Dip the cooled doughnuts into the glaze and return to the plate. Garnish with further chopped walnuts and serve.

White Chocolate Doughnuts

Ingredients

2 cups all-purpose flour

1 ½ teaspoons baking powder

½ teaspoon baking soda

½ teaspoon salt

2 eggs

½ cup sugar

¼ cup butter, melted

1 teaspoon vanilla

½ cup white chocolate chips

Glaze

1 cup confectioners' sugar

½ cup white chocolate chips

½ teaspoon vanilla

2 tablespoons milk

Instructions

Preheat oven to 350F. Add the flour, sugar, baking powder, baking soda and salt into a bowl and set aside. Add the eggs, butter and vanilla into a different bowl and whisk. Add the wet ingredients to the dry and mix in. Melt half a cup of chips, add to the mixture and stir in.

Add the dough to the pre-greased pan and cook for about 10 minutes. Let them cook in the pan for a couple of minutes and then remove to a wire rack. While cooling, make the glaze. Melt the remaining chips with the vanilla and milk in a glass bowl over boiling water and then whisk in the confectioners' sugar. Dip each cooled doughnut into the glaze and cover with more chips or a topping of your choice.

Printed in Great Britain
by Amazon